BREAKOUT BIOGRAPHIES

THE INVENTORS OF MINECRAFT

Markus "Notch" Persson and his Coding Team

Jill Keppeler

PowerKiDS press.

New York

MAR 2 0 2018

3 9082 13559 8418

Published in 2018 by The Rosen Publishing Group, Inc.
29 East 21st Street, New York, NY 10010

First Edition

Editor: Elizabeth Krajnik
Book Design: Tanya Dellaccio

Photo Credits: Cover PA Images/Yui Mok/Alamy Stock Photo; cover, back cover, pp. 1, 3, 4, 6, 8, 10, 12, 14, 16, 18, 20, 22, 24, 26, 28, 30–32 ninanaina/Shutterstock.com; p. 5 (top) Mike Prosser/www.flickr.com/photos/colmmcsky/8055591651/CC BY-SA 2.0; pp. 5 (bottom), 15 Christian Petersen/Getty Images News/Getty Images; p. 7 (top) Steven Saus/ www.flickr.com/photos/uriel1998/7991969276/ CC BY 2.0; p. 7 (bottom) Amy Johansson/ Shutterstock.com; p. 7 (Markus Persson) https://upload.wikimedia.org/wikipedia/commons/e/e5/ GDC_2016_awards_16-20_43_08-01-7D2_0752_%2825757405781%29.jpg; p. 9 (top) focal point/ Shutterstock.com; p. 9 (bottom) Andrew Harrer/Bloomberg/Getty Images; p. 11 Mike Prosser/www.flickr.com/photos/colmmcsky/14106106983/CC BY-SA 2.0; p. 13 (top) Wesley Fryer/www.flickr.com/photos/wfryer/15676438795/CC BY 2.0; p. 13 (bottom) Bloomicon/Shutterstock.com; p. 17 (top) www.flickr.com/photos/ s083027/9452694836/CC BY 2.0; p. 17 (bottom) Diego Gómez/www.flickr.com/ photos/129082387@N05/15379777193/CC BY 2.0; p. 17 (Jens Bergensten) https:// commons.wikimedia.org/wiki/File:Jens_Bergensten_Minecon.jpg; p. 19 (main) Rebecca Andrews/ REX Shutterstock/ASSOCIATED PRESS/AP Images; p. 19 (Lydia Winters) https://commons.wikimedia.org/ wiki/File:Lydia_Winters_-_Game_Developers_Choice_Online_Awards_(1).jpg; p. 21 (top) urbanbuzz/ Shutterstock.com; p. 21 (bottom) Karwai Tang/WireImage/Getty Images; p. 23 (top) Gabe Ginsberg/ FilmMagic/Getty Images; p. 23 (bottom) Chris Ratcliffe/Bloomberg/Getty Images; p. 25 (top) Worawee Meepian/Shutterstock.com; p. 25 (bottom) Monkey Business Images/Shutterstock.com; p. 27 Roberto Machado Noa/LightRocket/Getty Images; p. 29 (top) Yui Mok/EMPPL PA Wire/ Associated Press/AP Images; p. 29 (bottom) Casey Rodgers/Invision/Invision for Microsoft/AP Images.

Cataloging-in-Publication Data
Names: Keppeler, Jill.
Title: The inventors of Minecraft / Jill Keppeler.
Description: New York : PowerKids Press, 2018. | Series: Breakout biographies | Includes index.
Identifiers: ISBN 9781508160625 (pbk.) | ISBN 9781508160649 (library bound) | ISBN 9781508160632 (6 pack)
Subjects: LCSH: Persson, Markus, 1979–Juvenile literature. | Computer programmers–Sweden–Biography–Juvenile literature. | Minecraft (Game)–Juvenile literature. | Computer games–Design–Juvenile literature.
Classification: LCC HD8039.D372 K47 2018 | DDC 794.8092–dc23

Manufactured in China

CPSIA Compliance Information: Batch Batch #BS17PK: For Further Information contact Rosen Publishing, New York, New York at 1-800-237-9932

CONTENTS

THE STORY OF A GAME

Night is falling in the world of *Minecraft*.

As the sun sets over the hills, you hurry toward your little wooden house, iron sword in hand, keeping an eye out for all the creatures that come out after dark. You're almost there when you sense movement to your right. You look—and there's a strange, silent, green creature staring back at you. It starts to make a hissing noise.

Boom!

That scene might seem odd to those who haven't played *Minecraft*, one of the most popular video games of all time, but to those who have, it's very familiar. Much of that world can be traced back to one man, the game he dreamed up, and the team he put together to make that dream a reality. This man is Markus "Notch" Persson.

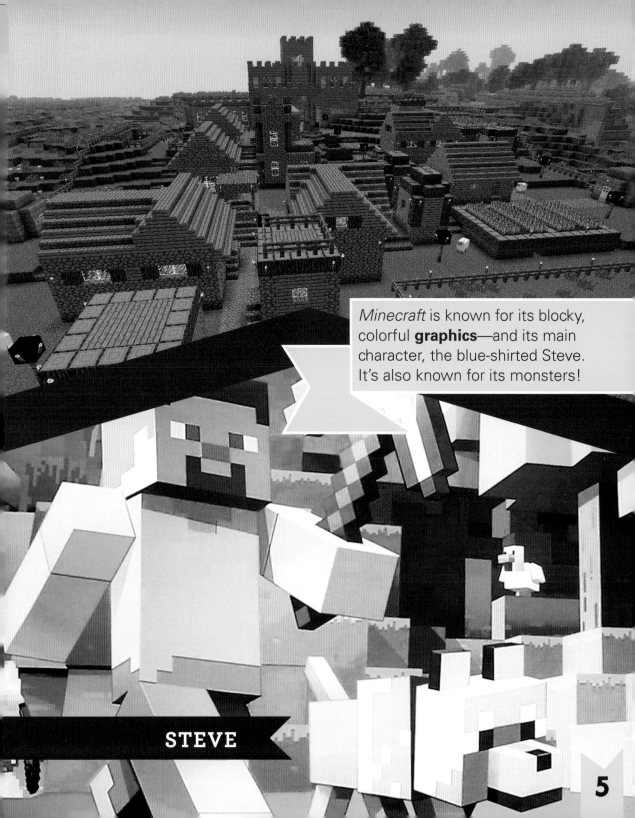

Minecraft is known for its blocky, colorful **graphics**—and its main character, the blue-shirted Steve. It's also known for its monsters!

STEVE

WHO IS NOTCH?

Markus Persson was born June 1, 1979, in Stockholm, Sweden. His father bought the family's first computer when Markus was seven years old. By the time he was eight, Persson had written his first computer program—a simple adventure game. At the time, though, he didn't plan a future in computers. He actually wanted to become a policeman.

When Persson was about 13 years old, he became friends with a number of other young programmers. They would compete to create the most interesting effects on their computers. By the time Persson was about 15, he had decided he wanted to have a career in creating computer games. His teachers, however, suggested that he learn how to create websites and he started studying graphic design.

Markus Persson lived in the town of Edsbyn, Sweden, until he was seven, when his family moved to Stockholm. The forests around Edsbyn may have influenced the scenery of *Minecraft*.

After high school, Persson worked for a small website company, but he quit after a short period of time. He took one class on the computer programming language C++ and continued to work on other projects. After a few years, he found a job with Gamefederation, which **distributed** video games.

In 2004, Persson went to work as a game programmer for a company called Midasplayer, which was later renamed King.com. Finally, he was working in the field he loved so much.

While there, he made another important connection. Persson befriended Jakob Porsér, who was a game developer at Midasplayer. That friendship would eventually lead to an important business partnership. Persson and Porsér started coding their own games in their spare time.

In 2005, Midasplayer became King.com. This company has created a number of famous games, including *Candy Crush Saga* and related titles.

JAKOB PORSÉR

Jakob Porsér has never been in the spotlight as much as Markus Persson has. Porsér was born on February 13, 1978, and started working at Midasplayer not long after Persson was hired. Porsér and Persson both liked to play collectible card games, which would be important in the future. Porsér enjoys another game as well. In February 2015, he became a main backer of the Luleå hockey team in Sweden.

CREATING
MINECRAFT

In 2009, Persson switched jobs again. He started working as a programmer for a company named jAlbum. He didn't work on games in this job, but it gave him more time to work on his own creations. He also made another important business connection with the company's **chief executive officer (CEO)**, Carl Manneh.

Not long after that, Persson started tinkering with a new computer game. Those playing this game would be able to explore and make changes to 3-D worlds and view the game's blocky graphics through the eyes of an **avatar**. He wrote the first code for that game in about a week. Soon, he posted a video online showing an early **version**. It drew a lot of interest and, not long after that, Persson gave his new game a name: *Minecraft*.

A number of earlier games inspired Markus Persson to create *Minecraft*. One of them was *Dwarf Fortress*, in which players manage a group of characters building a fortress. Everything in the game is represented by ordinary letters, numbers, and symbols.

In May 2009, Persson released the first playable version of *Minecraft* to a select group of people online. The response was positive and, in June, he released a version for sale. To his surprise, money starting rolling in as players **downloaded** it from his website.

By the summer of 2010, people had purchased more than 20,000 copies of *Minecraft*. The game soon made Persson a lot of money. And its popularity kept growing. In one 24-hour period in August 2010, more than 23,000 copies sold—more than in the entire previous year.

Through all this, Persson kept adding new features to the game. He quit his job at jAlbum to work on *Minecraft* full time. And he didn't do so alone. His old friend Jakob Porsér came to work with him.

Markus Persson didn't spend any money advertising *Minecraft*. Especially in the beginning, people found out about it through word of mouth, or hearing other people talk about it. ▶

IN THE WORLD OF *MINECRAFT*

While *Minecraft* has changed over the years, the general idea remains the same. Players can wander at will through **unique**, blocky worlds full of a variety of **environments** (from deserts to oceans to jungles) and creatures (from chickens to polar bears). In the creative setting, players have unlimited resources and can build and create whatever they can imagine. In other settings, they have to find their own resources—and deal with monsters, including zombies, skeletons, and the iconic creepers.

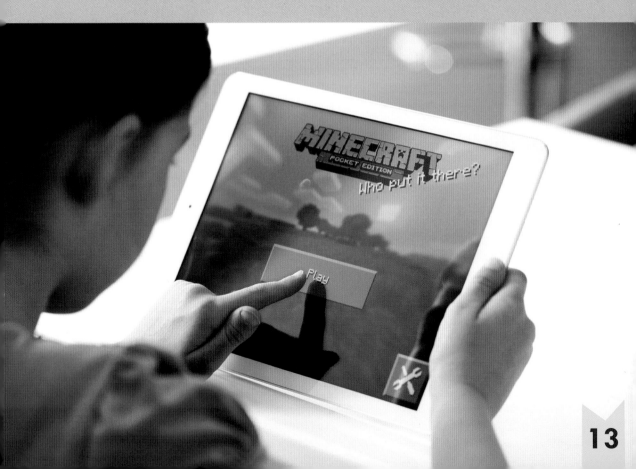

MOJANG

Persson and Porsér had wanted to start their own game development company for years. The two men met with Carl Manneh, the CEO of jAlbum and Persson's former boss, to discuss their dream. Soon, Manneh joined them in this venture.

In fall 2010, Mojang AB was born. The company was named after the Swedish word for **gadget**. Persson and Porsér were the owners of the new company and would handle the development of *Minecraft* and new games. Manneh would serve as the CEO and be in charge of the business side of things.

They found an office: a small apartment in Stockholm. Then it was time to start looking for Mojang's first employees. Persson would no longer have to juggle all things *Minecraft* by himself.

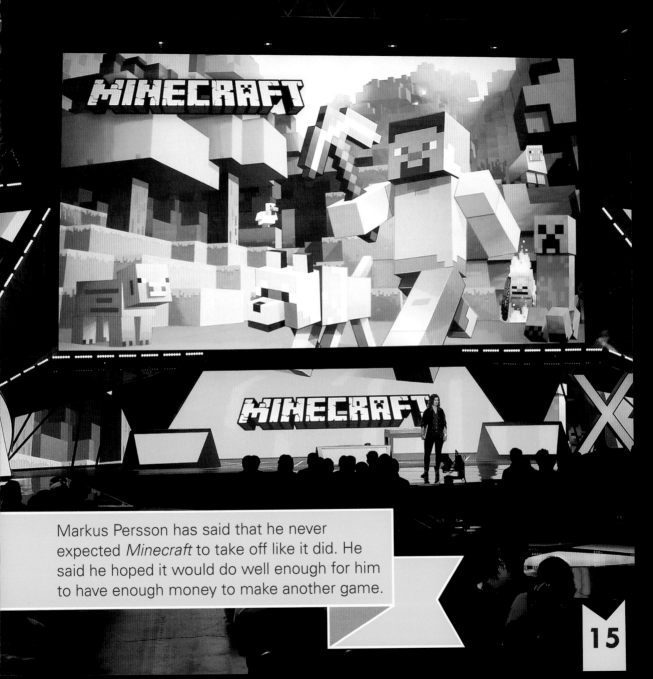

Markus Persson has said that he never expected *Minecraft* to take off like it did. He said he hoped it would do well enough for him to have enough money to make another game.

BUILDING

A TEAM

One of Mojang's first new employees was Jens "Jeb" Bergensten, a Swedish programmer. Bergensten, like Persson, became interested in creating games when he was about eight years old. He taught himself coding languages as a child and earned a master's degree in computer science.

At Mojang, Bergensten was actually hired to work on *Scrolls*, a new game that Porsér had planned. But *Scrolls* was still just an idea at that time, so Bergensten took a look at the *Minecraft* code instead. Over the Christmas holiday that year, when no one else was in the office, he started tinkering with the game. He programmed inky black squids into it and figured out a way that players could dye the *Minecraft* sheep different colors. Persson saw the changes and liked them. Now *Minecraft* had one more programmer

Next to Markus Persson, Jens Bergensten is probably the most well-known person associated with *Minecraft*.

JENS BERGENSTEN

THE STORY OF *SCROLLS*

If *Minecraft* was Persson's baby, *Scrolls* was Porsér's. The idea for the game started with the collectible card games Persson and Porsér liked to play. *Scrolls*, which Mojang first released in 2013, was a **fantasy** game in which players used the powers on "scrolls," which are much like the cards in a card game, to destroy objects or enemies. The game didn't become as popular as *Minecraft*, but many people played it until the game shut down in 2016.

Gradually, the Mojang team grew. Daniel Kaplan was hired as business developer. Programmer Aron Nieminen, who met Persson at Midasplayer, joined the crew as a game developer. Lydia Winters, who produced *Minecraft* YouTube videos under the name "MinecraftChick," was hired with the unique title "director of fun."

Many of these early employees at Mojang were (and still are) known by nicknames. At least one person, art director "Junkboy," whose real name is Markus Toivonen, is known mostly by his nickname. Kaplan is known as "Kappische." And Persson, of course, is known as "Notch."

By spring 2012, Mojang had 16 employees. That might not seem like very many, but for a company that started with one man and his creation, it was a lot.

MineCon, an annual *Minecraft* convention held by Mojang, draws thousands of *Minecraft* fans from around the world. MineCon 2015 was held in London, England. ▶

LYDIA
WINTERS

BLOCK
BY BLOCK

As the Mojang team was coming together, work on *Minecraft* continued. The finished version was released in November 2011 at the first MineCon event in Las Vegas, Nevada. By January 2012, people had purchased 1 million copies of the game. Just three months later, that number had doubled.

In May 2012, Mojang teamed up with Microsoft to release a version of *Minecraft* for the Xbox 360 gaming system. More versions followed. The LEGO group released its first set of blocks based on *Minecraft* in 2012. And *Time* magazine named Persson and Bergensten to its "100 Most Influential People" list in April 2013.

However, even as all this was going on, things were changing at Mojang. In December 2011, Persson had quietly stepped down as *Minecraft*'s lead developer. Bergensten had taken his place.

XBOX 360

MAKING *MINECRAFT* ACCESSIBLE

Minecraft is a game many people worldwide enjoy playing. Mojang wanted to make the game accessible, or available, to as many people as possible. Today, *Minecraft* is available on several platforms such as Xbox 360 and PlayStation. Although the versions of the game are similar from platform to platform, some platforms have special features such as in-game tutorials. This requires a lot of different types of programming and cooperation with designers!

Markus Persson has said that he enjoyed playing with LEGO bricks as a child. Today, children (and adults) can play with LEGO sets and bricks based on Persson's most famous creation.

Minecraft continued to grow. Mojang added new features and versions of the game. *Minecraft Realms* allows players to host their own game worlds for more than one player on Mojang **servers**. Companies produced more *Minecraft* **merchandise**, including books and toys.

Meanwhile, Persson started working on a few other things. One was an outer space game called *0x10c* (pronounced "zero times 10 to the C"). After he released some details of the game people became very excited. Persson was suddenly under a lot of pressure to finish it. Working on the game, he said later, was no longer fun.

In August 2013, Persson announced that he had stopped working on *0x10c*. Instead, he said, he just planned to work on smaller games for the rest of his life.

In addition to the game, people can buy all sorts of *Minecraft* merchandise now, from stuffed monsters to clothing to action figures.

BEGINNING OF THE END

More problems were brewing in the world of *Minecraft*. Many users hosted *Minecraft* games on servers of their own. Some of them made a lot of money out of these worlds. Some charged extra money for items that players could buy to help them in the game. This was against the game's license terms.

In early 2014, Mojang said that, while *Minecraft* servers and some in-game purchases would be allowed, the rules would now be enforced on items that gave some players an advantage. Many *Minecraft* players became very angry about this, and many sent Persson mean messages.

Eventually, Persson had enough. On June 16, 2014, he wrote, "Anyone want to buy my share of Mojang so I can move on with my life?" on Twitter.

Someone did.

Markus Persson and the other developers of *Minecraft* have been very active on social media such as Twitter. This means they can communicate with their fans, but it comes with problems too. Persson said later that he struggled with how mean some people can be online.

CYBERBULLYING

Cyberbullying is bullying that takes place using electronic devices, such as computers or smartphones. It can be text messages or e-mails, rumors that are spread online, embarrassing pictures, or other things sent or posted on the Internet. Sometimes people feel like they can say whatever they want when they're on a mobile device or behind a computer screen. But mean words can hurt people no matter how ordinary or famous they are. Even Markus Persson had to deal with cyberbullies.

THE SALE

Very soon after Persson's Twitter post, Mojang CEO Carl Manneh started receiving calls from companies that wanted to buy Mojang. On September 15, 2014, Mojang announced that American computer company Microsoft would buy it for $2.5 billion.

The day the deal was announced, Persson posted another message to fans online. In it, he wrote, "I love you. All of you. Thank you for turning *Minecraft* into what it has become, but there are too many of you, and I can't be responsible for something this big . . . .

"It's not about the money. It's about my **sanity**."

The sale became final in November 2014. Persson, Porsér, and Manneh left the company as soon as it was finalized.

In 2015, people play *Minecraft* inside a Microsoft store in the state of Washington. Persson had said in interviews that he would never sell Mojang to a big company, but he changed his mind because of issues with the game's fans.

MOVING ON

Several years after the sale, *Minecraft* continues to grow. Mojang and Microsoft have released the game on more systems and continue to add to it. In June 2016, Mojang announced that it had sold 100 million copies of *Minecraft* for computers, gaming systems, and mobile devices. People from every continent on Earth, including Antarctica, have purchased the game.

In an interview with the *Escapist* in August 2016, Persson said that he likes to balance his social life and his programming life. Persson said he feels "the most productive and happy" when he's alone and programming. He is able to use his time to continue learning new things and programming new games. Persson still wants to make "the best game [he] can make."

Markus Persson made the news about a month after he left Mojang when he bought a house worth $70 million in Beverly Hills, California. He has started a new company called Rubberbrain with Jakob Porsér, but it hasn't produced any games yet. Persson has remained active on social media, especially Twitter. He engages with his followers to keep up with gaming pop culture.

Today, *Minecraft* is big business. According to Mojang, if everyone who had purchased a copy of the game were part of one nation, it would be bigger than most countries in the world!

TIMELINE

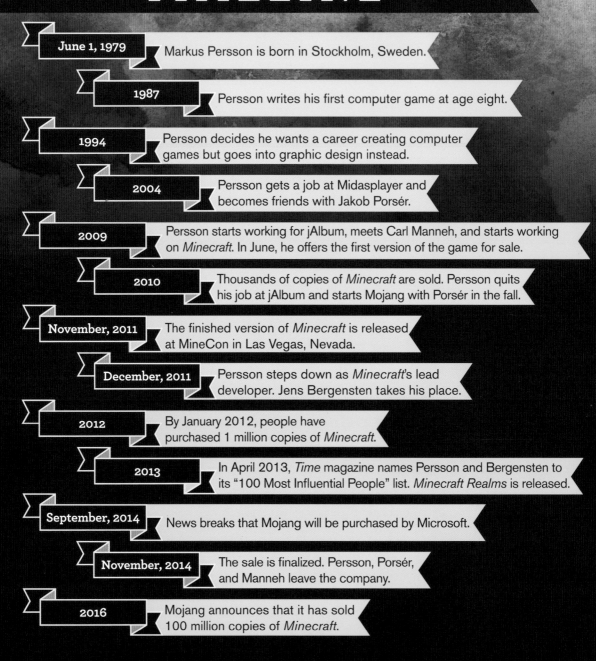

June 1, 1979 — Markus Persson is born in Stockholm, Sweden.

1987 — Persson writes his first computer game at age eight.

1994 — Persson decides he wants a career creating computer games but goes into graphic design instead.

2004 — Persson gets a job at Midasplayer and becomes friends with Jakob Porsér.

2009 — Persson starts working for jAlbum, meets Carl Manneh, and starts working on *Minecraft*. In June, he offers the first version of the game for sale.

2010 — Thousands of copies of *Minecraft* are sold. Persson quits his job at jAlbum and starts Mojang with Porsér in the fall.

November, 2011 — The finished version of *Minecraft* is released at MineCon in Las Vegas, Nevada.

December, 2011 — Persson steps down as *Minecraft*'s lead developer. Jens Bergensten takes his place.

2012 — By January 2012, people have purchased 1 million copies of *Minecraft*.

2013 — In April 2013, *Time* magazine names Persson and Bergensten to its "100 Most Influential People" list. *Minecraft Realms* is released.

September, 2014 — News breaks that Mojang will be purchased by Microsoft.

November, 2014 — The sale is finalized. Persson, Porsér, and Manneh leave the company.

2016 — Mojang announces that it has sold 100 million copies of *Minecraft*.

GLOSSARY

avatar: An image, such as one in a computer game, that represents and is controlled by a computer user.

chief executive officer (CEO): The person who has the most authority in an organization.

distribute: To share, sell, or otherwise spread something out.

download: To copy data from one computer to another, often over the Internet.

environment: Everything that is around a person.

fantasy: Something that is imagined and not real.

gadget: A small, useful device that is often interesting, unfamiliar, or unusual.

graphic: Having to do with pictures and shapes.

merchandise: Items that are bought and sold in business.

sanity: The state of having a healthy mind.

server: A computer or group of computers used by organizations for storing, processing, and distributing large amounts of data.

unique: Special or different from anything else.

version: A form of something that is different from the forms that came before it.

INDEX

WEBSITES

Due to the changing nature of Internet links, PowerKids Press has
developed an online list of websites related to the subject of this book.
This site is updated regularly. Please use this link to access the list:
www.powerkidslinks.com/bbios/persson